Garden Notes
This Year

For A Year Of Your Garden Notes...

Start writing on any date with this week-by-week layout. Record what blooms when; the names of your plants, birds that come to your feeder, and the progress, thoughts, and plans that develop during your year in the garden. The layout and structure make it easy. There are pages for garden visits, too.

Name_____

Place_____

Starting Date_____

ISBN 1-893443-13-2

B. B. Mackey Books
P. O. Box 475
Wayne, PA 19087-0475

www.mackeybooks.com
info@mackeybooks.com
'Something special in garden books.'

To reorder, write for information or go to our website.
Free book lists and order forms are available online
and also will be mailed to you on request.

Using this book, examples:

The Week of January 8 to January 14

Weather observations

    snow, 28 degrees

Bird and wildlife notes

    mourning doves appeared

Plant observations: growth, bloom, fruit...

    holly berries gone, eaten by birds.
    the cold frame is under snow, ok though.

Events this week:

    party at Mary's 6 pm Jan. 10
    Al here Jan. 9
    Joan's birthday Jan. 10
    full moon -- plant seeds

Seeds or plants planted or acquired:

    planted all--rudbeckia, gaura
    viola
    thai hot peppers

Tasks done, things to do:

    bought potting soil
    sent seed exchange form
    * Get new tubes for grow light!!

Weather observations:

Bird and wildlife notes:

Plant observations: growth, bloom, fruit...

The Week of January 1 to January 7

Events this week:

Seeds or plants planted or acquired:

Tasks done, things to do:

Weather observations:

Bird and wildlife notes:

Plant observations: growth, bloom, fruit...

The Week of January 8 to January 14

Events this week:

Seeds or plants planted or acquired:

Tasks done, things to do:

Weather observations:

Bird and wildlife notes:

Plant observations: growth, bloom, fruit...

The Week of January 15 to January 21

Events this week:

Seeds or plants planted or acquired:

Tasks done, things to do:

Weather observations:

Bird and wildlife notes:

Plant observations: growth, bloom, fruit...

The Week of January 22 to January 28

Events this week:

Seeds or plants planted or acquired:

Tasks done, things to do:

Weather observations:

Bird and wildlife notes:

Plant observations: growth, bloom, fruit...

The Week of January 29 to February 4

Events this week:

Seeds or plants planted or acquired:

Tasks done, things to do:

Weather observations:

Bird and wildlife notes:

Plant observations: growth, bloom, fruit...

The Week of February 5 to February 11

Events this week:

Seeds or plants planted or acquired:

Tasks done, things to do:

Weather observations:

Bird and wildlife notes:

Plant observations: growth, bloom, fruit...

The Week of February 12 to February 18

Events this week:

Seeds or plants planted or acquired:

Tasks done, things to do:

Weather observations:

Bird and wildlife notes:

Plant observations: growth, bloom, fruit...

The Week of February 19 to February 25

Events this week:

Seeds or plants planted or acquired:

Tasks done, things to do:

Weather observations:

Bird and wildlife notes:

Plant observations: growth, bloom, fruit...

The Week of February 26 to March 4

Events this week:

Seeds or plants planted or acquired:

Tasks done, things to do:

Weather observations:

Bird and wildlife notes:

Plant observations: growth, bloom, fruit...

The Week of March 5 to March 11

Events this week:

Seeds or plants planted or acquired:

Tasks done, things to do:

Weather observations:

Bird and wildlife notes:

Plant observations: growth, bloom, fruit...

The Week of March 12 to March 18

Events this week:

Seeds or plants planted or acquired:

Tasks done, things to do:

Weather observations:

Bird and wildlife notes:

Plant observations: growth, bloom, fruit...

The Week of March 19 to March 25

Events this week:

Seeds or plants planted or acquired:

Tasks done, things to do:

Weather observations:

Bird and wildlife notes:

Plant observations: growth, bloom, fruit...

The Week of March 26 to April 1

Events this week:

Seeds or plants planted or acquired:

Tasks done, things to do:

Weather observations:

Bird and wildlife notes:

Plant observations: growth, bloom, fruit...

The Week of April 2 to April 8

Events this week:

Seeds or plants planted or acquired:

Tasks done, things to do:

Weather observations:

Bird and wildlife notes:

Plant observations: growth, bloom, fruit...

The Week of April 9 to April 15

Events this week:

Seeds or plants planted or acquired:

Tasks done, things to do:

Weather observations:

Bird and wildlife notes:

Plant observations: growth, bloom, fruit...

The Week of April 16 to April 22

Events this week:

Seeds or plants planted or acquired:

Tasks done, things to do:

Weather observations:

Bird and wildlife notes:

Plant observations: growth, bloom, fruit...

The Week of April 23 to April 29

Events this week:

Seeds or plants planted or acquired:

Tasks done, things to do:

Weather observations:

Bird and wildlife notes:

Plant observations: growth, bloom, fruit...

The Week of April 30 to May 6

Events this week:

Seeds or plants planted or acquired:

Tasks done, things to do:

Weather observations:

Bird and wildlife notes:

Plant observations: growth, bloom, fruit...

The Week of May 7 to May 13

Events this week:

Seeds or plants planted or acquired:

Tasks done, things to do:

Weather observations:

Bird and wildlife notes:

Plant observations: growth, bloom, fruit...

The Week of May 14 to May 20

Events this week:

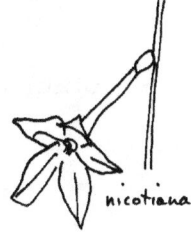

nicotiana

Seeds or plants planted or acquired:

Tasks done, things to do:

Weather observations:

Bird and wildlife notes:

Plant observations: growth, bloom, fruit...

The Week of May 21 to May 27

Events this week:

Seeds or plants planted or acquired:

Tasks done, things to do:

Weather observations:

Bird and wildlife notes:

Plant observations: growth, bloom, fruit...

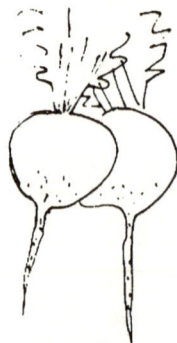

The Week of May 28 to June 3

Events this week:

Seeds or plants planted or acquired:

Tasks done, things to do:

Weather observations:

Bird and wildlife notes:

Plant observations: growth, bloom, fruit...

The Week of June 4 to June 10

Events this week:

Seeds or plants planted or acquired:

Tasks done, things to do:

Weather observations:

Bird and wildlife notes:

Plant observations: growth, bloom, fruit...

The Week of June 11 to June 17

Events this week:

Seeds or plants planted or acquired:

Tasks done, things to do:

Weather observations:

Bird and wildlife notes:

Plant observations: growth, bloom, fruit...

The Week of June 18 to June 24

Events this week:

Seeds or plants planted or acquired:

Tasks done, things to do:

Weather observations:

Bird and wildlife notes:

Plant observations: growth, bloom, fruit...

The Week of June 25 to July 1

Events this week:

Seeds or plants planted or acquired:

Tasks done, things to do:

Weather observations:

Bird and wildlife notes:

Plant observations: growth, bloom, fruit...

The Week of July 2 to July 8

Events this week:

Seeds or plants planted or acquired:

Tasks done, things to do:

Weather observations:

Bird and wildlife notes:

Plant observations: growth, bloom, fruit...

The Week of July 9 to July 15

Events this week:

Seeds or plants planted or acquired:

Tasks done, things to do:

Weather observations:

Bird and wildlife notes:

Plant observations: growth, bloom, fruit...

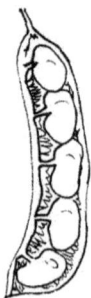

The Week of July 16 to July 22

Events this week:

Seeds or plants planted or acquired:

Tasks done, things to do:

Weather observations:

Bird and wildlife notes:

Plant observations: growth, bloom, fruit...

The Week of July 23 to July 29

Events this week:

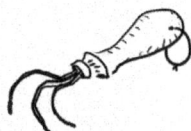

Seeds or plants planted or acquired:

Tasks done, things to do:

Weather observations:

Bird and wildlife notes:

Plant observations: growth, bloom, fruit...

The Week of July 30 to August 5

Events this week:

Seeds or plants planted or acquired:

Tasks done, things to do:

Weather observations:

Bird and wildlife notes:

Plant observations: growth, bloom, fruit...

The Week of August 6 to August 12

Events this week:

Seeds or plants planted or acquired:

Tasks done, things to do:

Weather observations:

Bird and wildlife notes:

Plant observations: growth, bloom, fruit...

The Week of August 13 to August 19

Events this week:

Seeds or plants planted or acquired:

Tasks done, things to do:

Weather observations:

Bird and wildlife notes:

Plant observations: growth, bloom, fruit...

The Week of August 20 to August 26

Events this week:

Seeds or plants planted or acquired:

Tasks done, things to do:

Weather observations:

Bird and wildlife notes:

Plant observations: growth, bloom, fruit...

The Week of August 27 to September 2

Events this week:

Seeds or plants planted or acquired:

Tasks done, things to do:

Weather observations:

Bird and wildlife notes:

Plant observations: growth, bloom, fruit...

The Week of September 3 to September 9

Events this week:

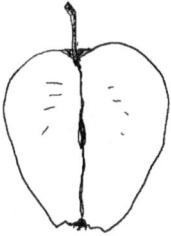

Seeds or plants planted or acquired:

Tasks done, things to do:

Weather observations:

Bird and wildlife notes:

Plant observations: growth, bloom, fruit...

The Week of September 10 to September 16

Events this week:

Seeds or plants planted or acquired:

Tasks done, things to do:

Weather observations:

Bird and wildlife notes:

Plant observations: growth, bloom, fruit...

The Week of September 17 to September 23

Events this week:

Seeds or plants planted or acquired:

Tasks done, things to do:

Weather observations:

Bird and wildlife notes:

Plant observations: growth, bloom, fruit...

The Week of September 24 to September 30

Events this week:

Seeds or plants planted or acquired:

Tasks done, things to do:

Weather observations:

Bird and wildlife notes:

Plant observations: growth, bloom, fruit...

The Week of October 1 to October 7

Events this week:

Seeds or plants planted or acquired:

Tasks done, things to do:

Weather observations:

Bird and wildlife notes:

Plant observations: growth, bloom, fruit...

The Week of October 8 to October 14

Events this week:

Seeds or plants planted or acquired:

Tasks done, things to do:

Weather observations:

Bird and wildlife notes:

Plant observations: growth, bloom, fruit...

The Week of October 15 to October 21

Events this week:

Seeds or plants planted or acquired:

Tasks done, things to do:

Weather observations:

Bird and wildlife notes:

Plant observations: growth, bloom, fruit...

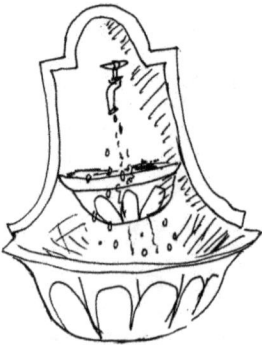

The Week of October 22 to October 28

Events this week:

Seeds or plants planted or acquired:

Tasks done, things to do:

Weather observations:

Bird and wildlife notes:

Plant observations: growth, bloom, fruit...

The Week of October 29 to November 4

Events this week:

Seeds or plants planted or acquired:

Tasks done, things to do:

Weather observations:

Bird and wildlife notes:

Plant observations: growth, bloom, fruit...

The Week of November 5 to November 11

Events this week:

Seeds or plants planted or acquired:

Tasks done, things to do:

Weather observations:

Bird and wildlife notes:

Plant observations: growth, bloom, fruit...

The Week of November 12 to November 18

Events this week:

Seeds or plants planted or acquired:

Tasks done, things to do:

Weather observations:

Bird and wildlife notes:

Plant observations: growth, bloom, fruit...

The Week of November 19 to November 25

Events this week:

Seeds or plants planted or acquired:

Tasks done, things to do:

Weather observations:

Bird and wildlife notes:

Plant observations: growth, bloom, fruit...

The Week of November 26 to December 2

Events this week:

Seeds or plants planted or acquired:

Tasks done, things to do:

Weather observations:

Bird and wildlife notes:

Plant observations: growth, bloom, fruit...

The Week of December 3 to December 9

Events this week:

Seeds or plants planted or acquired:

Tasks done, things to do:

Weather observations:

Bird and wildlife notes:

Plant observations: growth, bloom, fruit...

The Week of December 10 to December 16

Events this week:

Seeds or plants planted or acquired:

Tasks done, things to do:

Weather observations:

Bird and wildlife notes:

Plant observations: growth, bloom, fruit...

Events this week:

Seeds or plants planted or acquired:

Tasks done, things to do:

Weather observations:

Bird and wildlife notes:

Plant observations: growth, bloom, fruit...

The Week of December 24 to December 31

Events this week:

Seeds or plants planted or acquired:

Tasks done, things to do:

Notes on the Garden Year

Garden Visits

Garden Visitors

Thoughts for Next Year

❋❋❋

www.ingramcontent.com/pod-product-compliance
Lightning Source LLC
Chambersburg PA
CBHW031519040426
42445CB00009B/302